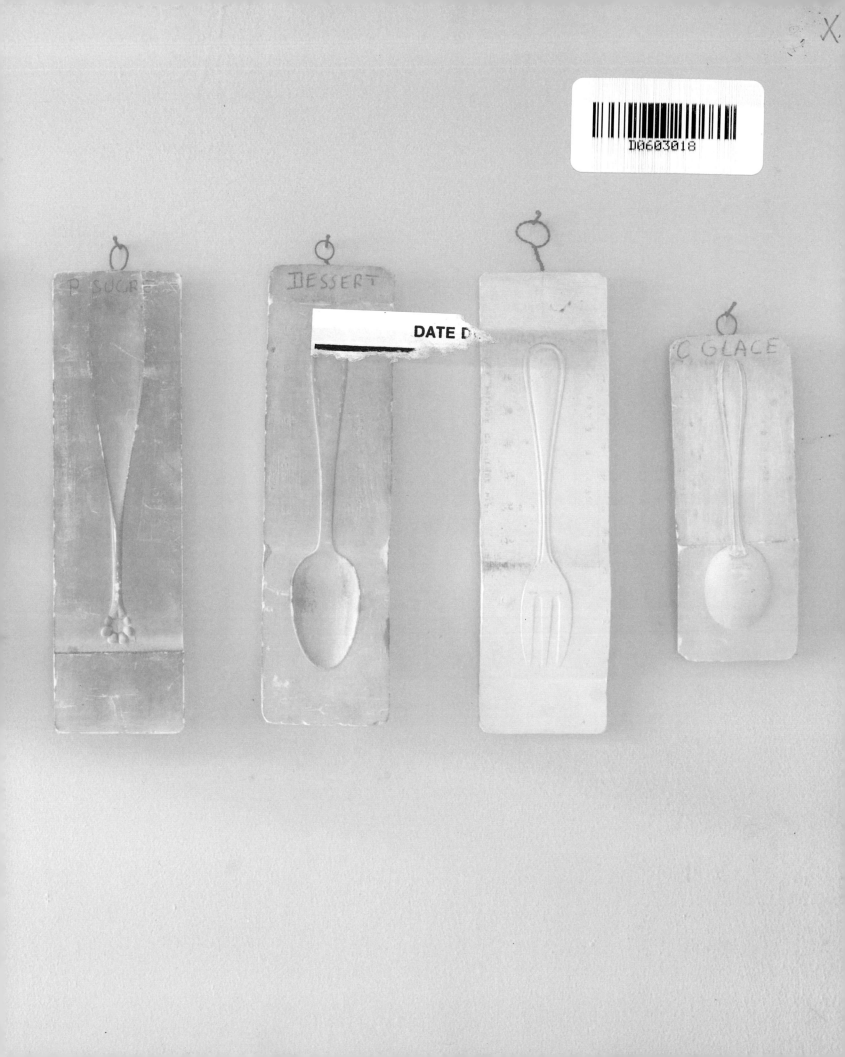

PERFECT TABLES

PERFECT TABLES

Tabletop secrets, settings, and centerpieces
for delicious dining

William Yeoward

PHOTOGRAPHY BY RAY MAIN

CICO BOOKS

LONDON NEW YORK

For Timothy

First published in 2006 by Cico Books
an imprint of Ryland, Peters & Small, Inc.
5th Floor, 519 Broadway
New York, NY 10012
Copyright © Cico Books Ltd 2006

Text copyright © William Yeoward 2006
Photographs © Cico Books 2006

10 9 8 7 6 5 4 3 2

A CIP catalog record for this book is available
from the Library of Congress

ISBN-10: 1-904991-53-X
ISBN-13: 978-1-9049-9153-3

Printed in China

Editor: Zia Mattocks
Designer: Chris Wood
Photographer: Ray Main

William Yeoward
270 Kings Road
London, UK SW3 5AW
+44 (0)20 7349 7828
www.williamyeoward.com

Contents

Introduction

Welcome to my book on table settings. Here, I reveal my secrets on creating the perfect table, covering a wide range of styles, themes, and occasions, from large parties to intimate gatherings, grand events to an informal supper. I have styled and set each one personally, so that I can share with you some of my ideas and experiences—from acquiring a good basic *mise en place* (set of plates and bowls) to the art of color-coordination and innovative decoration. A good host or hostess makes entertaining appear effortless, and I will impart some of the secrets that will help you to achieve this, whatever the occasion.

My passion for china, crystal, and glass goes back to my childhood, when I would spend my pocket money on vintage blue and white plates, search out pieces of fine linen, and marvel at the detailing of a Georgian knife handle or delicately cut piece of crystal. These still give me enjoyment and I delight in their individual and intrinsic beauty, as well as in seeing them grouped and arranged as part of a place setting.

Another great pleasure in my life is entertaining—friends, family, and business associates. To me, entertaining is far more than three courses and a glass of wine; it is about ambience, about putting people at their ease and creating an occasion that they will remember.

I often plan a menu while I'm at the market, when I can see what good, fresh ingredients are on offer. Once the courses are decided and the ingredients are purchased, I begin to think about the flowers. But the *pièce de résistance*, and what brings it all together, is the table setting. This is an art form in itself and one that will add to the pleasure you provide for your guests. If you delight in good food, wine, and company, then the creation of a table setting is a natural extension.

Not only will a skillfully arranged place setting enhance the appeal and appearance of the food you place on it, it will also show that you have taken time and trouble, that you cared enough about the people coming to your home to make that extra effort—to fold a table napkin in a certain way, for example, or to find an amusing napkin ring that will make them smile.

A well-dressed table doesn't have to be grand in style, but the setting should be appropriate to the occasion. Elaborate creations are wonderful for the right event—by all means dress your table to the nines if you are celebrating a significant birthday and the invitation states black tie or tuxedo—but for a special lunch with a close friend or afternoon tea with a dear relative, a simple and fun setting can help to create intimacy, a feeling of calm and relaxation, and even nostalgia.

Setting a table or even a tray need not be expensive or time-consuming; it is about editing and selecting the right accessories—things that are elegant, of good quality, and appropriate. Just a simple white linen cloth, a starched napkin, and a stylish crystal glass make a good starting point. Then simply fold the napkin, tie it with ribbon or cord, and add a single fresh flower and you have already created a visual treat. Have confidence to mix styles, colors, textures, and patterns, and try not to stick strictly to complete sets of matching glass and tableware. When everything matches exactly, the table will be dull and lacking in character. I often try out a single place setting before doing the whole table in the dining room. The trial setting provides an opportunity to test things, to mix and alter the plates and glasses until the right combination appears. It is like alchemy—there are endless combinations and inspirations to try, but finally you achieve the one that looks right for that night or special occasion.

In our increasingly busy lives it is important to find time for ourselves, our partners, and friends. Set aside a few hours to indulge in a leisurely breakfast, a picnic, or a simple lunch, and add a few extra moments of planning and arranging to make it an even more memorable occasion. You will be rewarded for your efforts and attention to detail. One of the greatest compliments is the look of delight and sometimes gasp of surprise from guests as they walk in and see, for the first time, the table set before them.

And remember that your setting, your interpretation of the arrangement of plates, glass, and flatware, is your own vision. You could give a group of people a table to set and they would all come up with a different result—it is all part of the fun.

I hope this book will help inspire you to turn everyday entertaining into a special occasion and even a simple supper into something memorable. Remember, there is no right or wrong, just your own opinion.

Enjoy,

CHAPTER ONE

Special Occasions

*From birthdays and Christmas to weddings
and anniversaries, here is a collection of
inspiring settings for every celebratory event,
for cozy gatherings and grand parties alike.*

left: Canvas director's chairs are comfortable enough to sit on for some time, as the canvas has a certain amount of give and the high back and arms provide adequate support. The chairs are also lightweight, are easy to move, and can be folded away to make room for dancing and to store after use.

right: The tables are arranged with plenty of space around them so that waiting staff can serve unhindered, but also so that the bride and groom, friends, and family can circulate easily and change places after the speeches.

A Floral
Wedding Breakfast

A family wedding is a time to celebrate, and to bring together friends and relatives that you may not have seen for some time. It is also an occasion when you will probably be introducing new people from another family to your own for the first time, so creating a relaxed atmosphere and providing ice-breaking conversation pieces are important aspects of the host's or hostess's duties.

This July wedding breakfast for 50 guests was held in a Raj-style tent in my country garden. It is at a lovely time of year when the flowers are in full bloom, so I used pale pink peonies, sweet peas, lavender, and rosemary cut from the borders and casually arranged in shiny vases to provide much of the decoration. The colors of these flowers are echoed by the rosé wine, the soft green and purple of the glasses, and the floral pattern of the tablecloths. Luckily, owing to the abundance of flowers growing in the garden, there were still plenty left to make the surroundings beautiful for guests who enjoyed drinks on the lawn before the wedding breakfast was served.

The tent provides shade and diffuses and softens the light that shines through the cream canvas. This type of tent is useful for a summer party because the side panels can be removed if the day is balmy and dry, to allow a cooling flow of air to circulate, and replaced if the weather is inclement, to protect the party from showers or cool gusts.

below left: A selection of tasty hors d'oeuvres will entice people to the table and encourage them to start a conversation by discussing the various layers and ingredients.

below: The informal arrangements of garden flowers help create a relaxed atmosphere, and their subtle fragrances are carried on the warm summer air. The peonies complement the blowsy blooms on the printed fabric used as tablecloths.

opposite: A tiered stand or tazza creates a dramatic and elegant centerpiece; it also adds height and scale to the table.

CREATING A CONVERSATION PIECE

When creating the setting for a party like this I always construct a focal point on the table, something people can comment on or discuss. For this summertime wedding breakfast I placed a tazza—a raised plate or dish—of tempting hors d'oeuvres on each table (see page 15). The tazza has long been associated with sweet foods and desserts, so using it for a colorful collection of savory hors d'oeuvres creates excitement and invites comment.

right: White and rosé wine and water decanted into stylish clear glass bottles can be placed at regular intervals along the length of each table, so that guests can easily help themselves.

opposite: Under the shade of the canvas tent awning, the tables have a relaxed and inviting feel. This is achieved by keeping plates and flatware to a minimum, with simple white china, a mixture of plain and colored glasses, loosely arranged garden flowers, and informal director's chairs.

below: To welcome guests back from the church and into the garden where the wedding breakfast is being held, a tray of glasses of chilled rosé and crisp white wine is offered.

An Unforgettable Birthday

Birthday festivities and parties can take many different guises. Sometimes the event is commemorated with a lavish dance, on other occasions with a surprise trip to a far-flung island, but most often birthdays are celebrated with an abundance of good food and wine shared with close friends—and where better than at your own table?

The friend whose birthday we celebrate here is a marvelous cook and an excellent host; a gathering at his home promises to be an evening of

above: The *grisaille* color of the bookcase is the perfect foil to tones of lavender, mauve, lilac, violet, fuchsia, and carnation pink. *Grisaille* is a French word describing a subtle shade of gray and is often heard in the expression "*Les grisailles du soir*," which translates, rather romantically, as "the grayness of the evening."

opposite: A trio of candlesticks punctuates the axis of the table between the two tall glass vases with their abundant floral displays. The candlelight reflects off the crystal glasses and makes the gilt edges of the plates glow.

unforgettable food and witty conversation with interesting people. He is also a well-traveled and widely read gentleman with a keen eye for fashion, so the elegant library doubles perfectly as an intimate and stylish dining room.

The wall of gray-painted bookcases, mirror-framed picture, and dimmable lighting provide an excellent background to this sumptuous setting. The rich dark wood of the tables is complemented by the striking chocolate brown plates with their wide gold rims. Deep pink, lilac, and dusky lavender tones are introduced through the floral displays and the napkins—as well as by the decadent fruit mousses served in champagne flutes. Lots of sparkling crystal glints in the candlelight, while a humorous note is added by the cashmere knitted "pastries." A dusk-to-dawn dinner such as this, held at a weekend so there is plenty of time to indulge and recover, really can't be improved upon.

below left: The chic chocolate and gold plates form the perfect platform for this elegant feast. Classic white linen napkins are given a novelty twist with these knitted "pastries."

below: Deep pink carnation heads in simple little glasses bring one of the main color accents to tabletop level.

opposite left: A wide-rimmed champagne flute makes a perfect serving dish for a fruit mousse.

opposite right: Unusual éclairs and tarts provide amusement to lighten the heart and the eye—after all, cashmere is not normally found fashioned in this form.

MIXING YOUR FRIENDS

If you are worried about your mixture of guests or those who don't know each other, make the table a little smaller than normal or set places closer together. It is an essential part of a good host's job to introduce people who come alone or do not know other guests. You should be well briefed as to who guests are and what they do, so that when you make an introduction you can start by giving a point of interest or something that the people being introduced will have in common, thereby giving them a subject on which to strike up conversation. Make the cocktails a little more exciting and *voilà*, success will be yours.

An Easter Table

Easter is a time of celebration and hope, marking the end of winter and the beginning of spring. Among the great joys of this time is the abundance of flowers, such as narcissi, hyacinths, and tulips, which can be gathered by the armful, and the promise of longer days lifts the spirits.

I dressed this celebration table with a dear friend, who was having a gathering of friends and family for Easter lunch. As the guests ranged in age from her grandmother to a young niece, we decided to add a dash of humor and an element of surprise with amusing napkins rings, hidden chocolate eggs, and tiny festive toys.

opposite: This table is full of unexpected treats, with little toy animals and chocolates nestling among the flowers, plates, and glasses. I chose wine glasses with a mid-blue rim to echo the border of the plates.

right: Harry the hare watches over proceedings atop his napkin.

To complement the grand scale of this lovely dining room and its well-proportioned windows dressed with elegant draperies, I devised a scheme that would take the flowers right up high. As one enters the room the two arrangements of mimosa and tulips in the very tall, slender glass vases are in perfect symmetry with the casement windows and in balance with the beautiful crystal chandelier that hangs above the table.

CREATING FLORAL DISPLAYS

The main rule for arranging flowers for a table is that the display should be either above or below the eye level of people conversing across the table. The guests should be able to have direct eye contact with the person they are talking to without having to duck up and down or around the flowers. When you are using glass or crystal vases, remember that it isn't just the flower heads that are on show—you'll see the stems as well, so they should be clean, neatly cut, and placed in clear water. I always try to find flowers that are in season. Forced flowers don't last, and one of the nice things about holding a party at home is that you can have the pleasure and enjoyment of the flowers during the following days.

previous page: The table is centered beneath the chandelier with a graduated floral "hill" arrangement beneath. The two very tall vases of flowers on either side stand directly in front of the casement windows.

below left: Copious quantities of family silver make dressing a table a delight, but it should always be polished before it is set on the table. You can make the shine last longer by storing silverware in airtight bags.

below center: Crystal cellars can be used as miniature vases to hold a few beautiful buds or flower heads at low level.

below: Mid-nineteenth-century Masons Ironstone plates are found in many a well-stocked china closet.

opposite: Sugar-coated chocolate eggs in a marvelous crystal urn vie with the narcissi for attention. Cut glass and crystal sit comfortably on any table and with any type of flower.

Anniversary Dinner for Thirty

I threw a smart party in my London apartment to celebrate the tenth wedding anniversary of a really wonderful and dear couple of close friends. Because the number of guests invited could not be accommodated comfortably in my dining room, I took all the furniture out of the more spacious sitting room and transformed it into a dining space. I hired elegant banqueting chairs with purple seats and floor-length undercloths to match, and set them around three circular tables, each of which could seat ten guests.

As space was restricted I kept the centerpieces compact but tall. I used a footed compote as a first tier, dressed with stout cream church candles, orchids, and fruit, and in the center placed a tall, slim fluted vase, which created a second tier, filled with long stems of foliage and flowers.

opposite: Three round tables provided comfortable seating for 30 guests in the sitting room. Keeping the color palette simple and the table decorations tall and slim prevented it from feeling crowded.

top right: Highly decorative crystal glasses sparkle in the candlelight and add glamour to the table.

right: A deep amethyst water glass picks up the color scheme and makes even a simple glass of water seem luxurious and opulent.

On the table at the base of each stand I arranged votive candles in low amethyst bowls hewn from rock crystal to give a glow of color and sparkle. The purple napkins were simply tied with burgundy satin ribbon. Dinner plates with decorative borders in two different patterns but toning colors have been used. The rich pinks, purples, and greens found in these plates were the inspiration for the colors of the chair cushions, undercloths, napkins, flowers, and fruit, giving an overall harmony and jewel-like richness to the room.

CREATING AMBIENCE WITH CANDLELIGHT

A well-dressed table is the star of the show and should always be the focus of attention as you enter the room. In the evening, this is easily achieved by dimming the ambient electric lighting so that the majority of the room is in shadow, and drawing attention to the table with an appropriate number of candles. If the room is a different color to those used on the table, casting soft shadows in this way makes this less noticeable. Candlelight is undeniably flattering to all skin tones and will also reflect off polished silver and crystal, making it glow and sparkle.

below left: Stemmed crystal is perfect for serving desserts such as fruit compotes, mousse, sorbet, or zabaglione. A few elegant crisp cookies and chocolate-dipped candied fruit are all the dressing that is needed.

below: A small portion of a very rich dessert, such as an intense chocolate soufflé, can be grandly displayed on an oversized plate, with a small "saucer" of crème anglaise or a drizzle of cream acting as a frame and highlighting the center of attraction.

opposite: Twinkling amethyst votives add extra glamour to the table decorations in pink and lavender tones, which are balanced by plain cream candles and an abundance of crystal.

A Family Thanksgiving

Thanksgiving is a time of joyous celebration and remembrance, an occasion when family and close friends gather around the table. Because of the importance of looking back to the past, I set the table with antique and vintage items that have history and memories, such as my great-grandmother's side plates, my grandmother's silver candlesticks, and silverware from my mother's canteen. But Thanksgiving is also a cheerful time, and each year I like to add a new and frivolous touch, such as the raffia and wooden napkin rings in the shapes of turkeys and reindeer.

The background to the setting is a plaid cloth in deep and light blue with fine yellow and orange stripes running through; it makes a wonderful foil for the silver and crystal that gleam and glint in the candlelight. From the abundance of late autumn flowers and burnished foliage I selected amaryllis, not only because these statuesque flowers add height to the table but also because their strong colors are found in both the cloth and the plates.

above left: Novelty napkin rings can help guests relax and offer a good opening for conversation.

left: Good-quality cut-crystal glasses will always make good wine taste even better.

opposite: Amaryllis is especially suitable for a table decoration because it has virtually no scent, so does not overpower or interfere with the aromas and flavors of the food.

previous page: The plaid fabric used as a tablecloth could allude to a family's Scottish heritage, but may also be used for traditional Scottish occasions such as Hogmanay and Burns Night. The regular linear pattern and harmonious hues of plaid make it a delightful backdrop to many schemes and arrangements. The quantity of crystal used here creates a feeling of abundance, but the table doesn't appear overcrowded because the transparency of crystal and glass doesn't block the flow of light.

opposite: A sideboard adjacent to the main table is a useful place to put decanters and serving spoons and forks, as well as other accessories. By keeping these pieces off the main table, you prevent it from becoming cluttered.

right: A small compote of nuts, dried figs, and chocolate-covered candied citrus peel is a decorative addition to the table as well as an alternative to the main dessert.

below left: Mixing antique and vintage family pieces with contemporary china, crystal, and amusing accessories makes an original setting for a special family gathering.

below right: For annual events such as Thanksgiving, I like to introduce a new element to my table setting each year. Some time ago, while I was on a business trip to Chicago, I came across these turkey napkin rings and bought them immediately—although Thanksgiving was months away, I instantly knew that they were worth buying and keeping.

Gilded Christmas

As so much of Christmas is focused on the younger members of the family, I like to hold a Christmas Eve dinner just for the grown-ups. When the children have gone to bed and the house is quiet, I begin my favorite Christmas ritual: setting the table with the most beautiful and beloved items from my china cupboard.

For this dinner party, I found gold in ninteenth-century embossed gilt flatware, a laurel-leaf candelabra, and shimmering, gold-rimmed wine glasses. Specially commissioned, handmade Christmas crackers filled with gifts are covered with crinkled paper reminiscent of fabulous Fortuny evening gowns. Finally, I have gold almond dragées cascading from cranberry glass chests with ormolu mounts; these add more than a touch of decadence and opulence to a glittering *mise en place*.

right: Never be scared of opulence; I am a firm believer that quality never dates. When entertaining at Christmas, be sure to use the best wares you possess.

opposite: An ethereal organdy bow with an explosion of wired pearls and custom-made crackers with pearl clusters follows the decorative theme and adds even more glamour to the table.

MAKING MORE OF A TABLE

To entertain a larger number of guests at home, or to give myself more room for a generous centerpiece, I extend my table using a false tabletop. The tabletop is simply a piece of unpainted board covered with green felt baize that I place over my smaller table for an instant table extension.

previous: For this occasion my table has been extended with a false top (see above) and to seat the number of invited guests I have brought chairs from other rooms to create a harlequin set. The table setting is a mix of the contemporary and traditional, brought together by the classic arrangement of flowers.

opposite: I love to add an unexpected dash of color to an elegant, gilded table. Here, the cranberry glass chests bring an element of surprise as their ormolu mounts complement the gold of the abundant almond dragées.

right: Be generous at Christmas; at this time of year I bring out my most treasured possessions, such as this nineteenth-century Irish wine pitcher.

below left: Not all wine glasses have to have long stems – fashions and trends change, and so can your choice of glasses. In the seventeenth and eighteenth centuries glasses tended to be more squat and robust, whereas finer, more elegant styles were in vogue in later eras.

below right: This candle, partly submerged in a vase of water, is surrounded with flowers so that the stems as well as the blooms become part of the decoration.

opposite: The stone-topped console with flowers and a Sèvres *sorbetière*, a period dish used for serving sorbet and ice cream.

below: The magnificent crystal centerpiece, which has a folded-over lip with a dentil-cut edge, is filled with passion fruits and grapes that carry on the amethyst accent color.

A Grand Gala

During the summer I am often invited to outdoor concerts and theater performances at country houses, many of which are combined with pre- or post-performance dinners that make the evening a gala event. With gentlemen in black tie and dinner jacket and ladies in fine summer gowns, it is a time to indulge the most sumptuous of table settings.

I was lucky enough to be invited to join the party at a house where an operetta was being performed. The house, an eighteenth-century brick building in beautiful landscaped grounds, is often referred to as "the greatest doll's house in Britain," and the hostess owns an incredible and venerable Sèvres porcelain dinner service.

Down the center of the table I have placed a long, oval Charles X *place surtout* made of mirror with ormolu gallery mounts. It comes in four sections that may be removed or added to suit the size of the table. As dusk falls, the mirrored surface will reflect and amplify the candlelight and become a lake of reflected light, which was the original purpose of the *place surtout* in the time before electric light was invented. It always makes me think of the Palace of Versailles and its marvelous mirrored *chambres*. The table is arranged in a classic format, with the centerpiece being the tallest item on the table and the most eye-catching. The oversized and well-spaced dining chairs automatically add to the feeling of opulence and luxury, while an abundance of sparkling crystal brings its own magical charm.

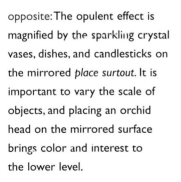

opposite: The opulent effect is magnified by the sparkling crystal vases, dishes, and candlesticks on the mirrored *place surtout*. It is important to vary the scale of objects, and placing an orchid head on the mirrored surface brings color and interest to the lower level.

right: Food can be used as an effective and decorative way of embellishing the table. This dish of dried apricots, cranberries, and chocolates on a cut-crystal compote provides temptation as well as decoration.

Inspired by the classical architecture and the yellow of the Sèvres porcelain, I created a table setting that was rich in embellishment and classic in style. I chose amethyst as the accent color and an off-white coffee-flecked damask cloth as a backdrop, its baroque pattern complementing the décor of the room.

In the eighteenth century, tables were set with less flatware than today, so I followed that dictate and kept the settings minimal, the flatware being replaced with each course. On occasions such as this, when dress is formal, I use extra-large napkins, so there's no risk of a disastrous accident.

below left: The mirrored *place surtout* makes a wonderful frame for the opulent table accessories and decorations.

below: Simple, elegant flatware encourages the eye to enjoy the beautiful antique porcelain. Crystal cellars can be used for both salt and ground pepper, with several placed at intervals along the length of the table.

below: Individual vases are grouped together with a bell-edged compote dish filled with unusual candies.

below right: The spires of Rome, Florence, and Paris seem to be suggested by this ravishing collection of decanters and covered vessels.

THE COMFORT FACTOR

There is nothing worse than your legs going numb from sitting on a hard seat, so make sure your dining chairs are comfortable and well upholstered—and if not, add a cushion. Chairs should be a good weight—sturdy but not too heavy to pull to the table or push back. A chair should also be the correct height in relation to the table, so that the person sitting on it can easily reach the table. Antique chairs bring elegance and history to a room, but they can be fragile and are often lacking in the upholstery department. Reproduction chairs can still capture something of a classic style and have all the advantages of modern manufacturing and good dense padding. I like to create visual diversity by mixing solids and patterned covers.

A colorful and humorous table arrangement has been made using vintage cloths and cake stands for a fun-filled teatime party.

Fun for Kids

Needlework was the inspiration behind the fun setting created for this children's tea party. It all started with the colorful crocheted bed cover that I grew up with, which I laid over a well-scrubbed kitchen table. Picking up on the vintage feel of the cloth, I added 1950s napkins and embellished them with pom-pom hair ties, which the girls took home as presents at the end. Although some people regard table napkins as old-fashioned, I think they are an essential part of any table—even for children. Jammy fingers and chocolate-smeared lips can be easily wiped clean if each child has their own napkin.

The colorful theme of the crocheted tablecloth was carried through with multicolored sprinkles lavishly scattered over the tops of sticky buns, and candy decorations dotted over the chocolate cake. My approach when catering for a children's party is to give the children the kind of food they enjoy and understand—it won't upset their nutritional balance to have custard tarts, chocolate cake, and cookies once in a while. As all the food can be eaten with fingers, the plates and cups are kept to a minimum, leaving more room for the fun things— toys and cakes.

Not all of the food on the table is real, however—some of the cookies, cakes, tarts, and candies are knitted. This joke food interspersed among the copious quantity of delicious edible treats caused peals of laughter from both the children and their parents and made the whole party an unforgettable event.

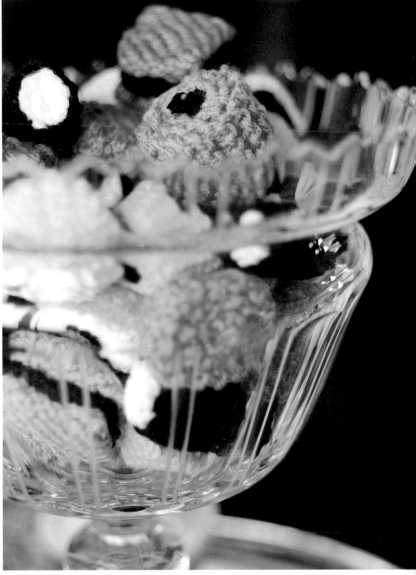

above right: Although the children who came to this party found the colorfulness of the theme and the toys fun, many of their parents remarked that it was reminiscent of their own childhood. There were many nostalgic memories of homemade jam and frosted cupcakes.

above: Colorful knitted "cakes" are dotted among the real things—this adds to the impression of volume without having to overcater and provides the fun of hide-and-seek for the edible delights.

opposite: A knitted tart nestles beside two real cookies topped with multicolored sprinkles. A mischievous mouse looks on from beneath a vintage glass cake stand.

VINTAGE NAPKINS

Vintage table napkins can be found in many antiques shops and stalls, and there are also a number of companies who produce modern sets with old-fashioned prints. Don't worry if you can't source a complete set of six or twelve matching napkins, as you can always bump up the number by adding solid-color ones in one of the shades featured in the print or pattern. If you can't find an exact match, you can always buy some good-quality cotton in a harmonizing shade, cut squares to the desired size, and hem them yourself.

CHAPTER TWO

Family & Friends

I love entertaining—bringing together friends and family for good food and conversation. The secret is to make it seem as though you've made more effort than you actually have.

A Woodland Picnic

This is the sort of picnic I take to summer opera festivals, outdoor concerts, or for a leisurely afternoon spent watching the regatta from the riverbank; it is smart and inviting but the dressings and accessories are limited by the knowledge that everything has to be carried. These informal summer outings are when I can really relax and enjoy myself. If possible, I like to add to my comfort by taking a folding table and chairs with me because I dislike trying to eat and drink while propping myself up on one elbow—it always ends in disaster.

I always select robust glasses that won't break easily and that have a good wide base to provide balance on an uneven surface. Some of the glasses

left: For outdoor entertaining, use the weightier styles of glasses, bowls, and stands with good broad bases that can be securely set on grass or blankets.

right: Although a picnic may be set in a grassy glade, it is always worth adding a small handful of freshly gathered flowers.

shown here are in attractive shades of lavender and moss green which enhance the feeling of indulgence and complement the fresh colors of the natural surroundings. Clear crystal and glassware has a light, ethereal presence, which suits the ambience of a sunny summer's day. Although you may be restricted by what is practicable to carry, there is no excuse for letting standards drop, so follow the rule that it is best to keep things natural, simple, and beautiful.

opposite: Trailing foliage and leafy tendrils can soon clutter up an indoor dining table, but a few fallen petals and leaves add to the relaxed and tranquil feel of a summer picnic.

below left: During the summer I like to use blowsy full-blown flowers, when they are at the peak of their beauty and their scent is at its strongest.

below center: Mint, borage, and lemon verbena look attractive in a pitcher of lemonade or fruit cup, as well as adding a fresh taste.

below: I usually use colored glasses to serve water, reserving the clear ones for wine.

SUMMER CUP: GRANNY'S SLAMMER

At my summer picnics and parties I like to serve a punch or cup as an alternative to straight wine or bar drinks. A cup is a low-alcohol drink that can be exquisitely tasty and refreshing without knocking your socks off. One of my favorites is Granny's Slammer. Mix a bottle of champagne with an equal quantity of chilled cranberry juice. Add a few thin strips of orange zest and serve over crushed ice. It's lighter and more unusual than straight champagne.

opposite: This tartan blanket is the ideal solution for an informal supper table, and I used it as inspiration for the rest of the setting. Its subtle, heathery colors dictated the palette of delicate creams and shades of purple and deep blue that I have used. Remember, you can never have too many salt and pepper sets—all the guests should be able to reach one easily.

right: Simple string works well as a casual napkin tie and is fitting for a kitchen supper.

Tartan Supper

I love spending the weekend pottering in the kitchen and around the garden, so Friday night supper is always a good but simple table—with no fuss but lots of style, naturally. This table is really all about making my friends feel that I've made an effort for them but without making them feel intimidated after a long week. Traveling as I do subjects me to endless different and varied situations, so I was gripped when visiting a friend of mine

in New England, who, preparing for a gathering of family and local chums, threw an old tartan blanket on her table with the exclamation, "Honey, I hate ironing! And surely the point of a great table is change." So, with the addition of a set of sparkling glasses and some elegant china, your entertainment centerpiece is made in minutes. Focus on layering up color, texture, and contrast, with a touch of novelty, then just add a bottle of good wine for simple style in minutes, with added time to relax.

above left: Miniature vintage glass butter pails find new life as tiny bud vases for single purple anemones; one is placed at each setting.

above: The vibrant blue square-based glasses and salt cellars pick up the darker indigo tones in the rug and really hold the look together.

opposite left and right: The earthy studio pottery, the linen napkin tied with string, and the horn-handled flatware all add new layers of tone and texture and are totally in keeping with the rustic atmosphere of this table setting.

ESSENTIAL POINTS TO CONSIDER

It's only when I'm driving home from shopping at our farmer's market for an informal weekend dinner that I know the menu—it all depends on what's on offer. One really can't set a table before choosing the food, as the courses and colors have a great influence on the look, so only then can I run through how the table will look. Use this checklist to make your own choices.

CLOTH: Yes or no and which style to choose?

NAPKINS: Linen, cotton, solid, or printed?

GLASS: Vintage or new? Must it be suitable for the dishwasher or will you wash by hand?

PLATES: Studio or simple? Shape and color?

FLATWARE: Everyday or smart silver?

LIGHTING: Always candles and votives, but what style and color holders?

FLOWERS: Cut flowers or plants or both, and with fruit and decorative vegetables, too?

above: Because of the many different but toning colors found in tartan cloth, it makes a great starting point for the color scheme of a table setting. This example, with earthy brown and terra-cotta stripes, creates a vibrant look when paired with fresh leaf-green dishes.

left: Every piece on the table is in one of the many rich tones found in the tartan weave. Matching the pale cream of the rough wool to the glossy glazed dishes and soft purple figs gives luxury to a simple snack. When you're planning tables, think texture—food—color, all at once. But add a little bit of flexibility; this table would also work rather well if we had been starting our supper with a tomato salad.

opposite: This delightful combination works because all the textures and colors are tonal and balanced. And the style levels work, too, with an old, grand Bristol blue water goblet next to the new, rustic wine glass.

opposite: A couple of comfortable chairs and a simple table can be arranged in a location other than the dining room. Here, I have created an intimate and different dining space on a landing.

right: A perfect white rose expresses love just as sincerely as a traditional red one.

below right: To change the look, I sometimes introduce a few pieces of unusual flatware, such as this spoon, with matching fork, made of polished coconut shell. This provides an unexpected contrast with the fine crystal.

With Love

This simple, measured setting is perfect for a Valentine supper—it isn't necessary to cover everything with red to get the message across. Here, the white roses and tall stems of tuberoses are enough to convey a heartfelt message. You could also use a setting like this for a farewell or *bon voyage* meal for a close friend; as a way of saying thank you for a special favor; or even to make a good impression on a first dinner date at home.

The muted and natural earthy shades of the tabletop and tableware are brought to life with vivid white napkins and flowers, with hints of fresh green. On the gently furled napkin a small, ceramic token makes a charming statement.

left: A few stems of tuberoses in three separate vases of different heights bring a lively dynamic to a simply set table.

below: A classic French *pot au chocolat* is used to serve soup; the lid helps to keep the contents of the pot warm while being transported to the table.

opposite: Raising food up from the table makes it appear exciting. These simple glass stands holding cheese and grapes and decorated with roses add elegance and grandeur.

CREATING AN INTIMATE SETTING

An intimate lunch or supper for just two is easy to transport to a new and less predictable setting, so take a table and a couple of chairs to another part of your home for a different view on life. On a sunny spring day you could position them by a window overlooking the garden or in the winter by a roaring fire in a study or den. Use your imagination to get out and beyond the conventional setting of the dining room or kitchen. A major part of the art of entertaining is creating the element of surprise.

left: Brightly colored Jello desserts in attractive glass dishes can be stacked in a tier to create variety and interest on the serving table.

opposite: The village hall has a stock of practical enamel plates trimmed with blue bands, which are ideal for this sort of entertaining. Although plain, they can be dressed up with pretty napkins. These were made by a local seamstress, who added deep borders of leftover gingham to discontinued floral-print handkerchiefs to produced a unique set.

Come Join the Party

Every year a lunch is held in the village hall near my home in the country. It is a real community occasion, with villagers ranging in age from nine months to 90 all coming together. Because the event has been going on for years, there are certain traditions and customs to be followed—for example, the menu consists of local food cooked to family recipes, and the flowers are a joyful mixture of blooms harvested from the surrounding cottage gardens. The challenge is to make the whole affair even better than the year before.

The theme and "palette" for this village lunch creates a nostalgic atmosphere that conjures up a time gone by; the colors are sunny and bright, which instantly conveys a feeling of happiness and optimism. There is a cheerful utilitarian red and white gingham cloth on the buffet table and a long length of inexpensive multicolored cotton seersucker spread over the main table. The seersucker was bought from a small neighborhood store and the ends were hemmed by a kindly local soul. All that's missing is the festive bunting.

below left: A side table helps to relieve the pressure for space on the main table. Pies, pickles, and extra salads can be arranged and kept here until needed for second helpings or to cater for late arrivals.

below: Because this lunchtime party inevitably carries on through the afternoon, we have an urn of hot water so that refreshing and reviving cups of tea can be served. Tea is made in a series of vintage pots so that it is always freshly brewed and tasty.

opposite: Instead of formal place cards I used small self-adhesive stationery labels stuck on the handles of the knives to indicate people's places. They can be peeled off before the knives are washed.

MIXING PATTERN

Linear patterns such as checks and stripes can be paired to great effect. Florals or paisleys can be added to the mixture, as long as the patterns share similar tones. Placing patterned fabric with plains prevents the look from being too busy.

above: Although the table setting is simple, I would never use picnic or plastic knives, forks, and spoons. To me it is essential to use conventional flatware, and it really only takes a few minutes to wash and dry it afterward.

left: Everyone contributes something to this party—from jars of pickles to bunches of flowers. It is impossible to predict what kind of vessels and vases will be needed, but here a collection of earthenware pitchers fits the bill.

opposite: Plain tableware can be dressed up with plenty of fresh flowers and food.

previous page: The sense of being part of a village is important to this occasion, and setting the table symbolizes the bringing together of the whole community.

For a simple setting such as this, I invariably focus on the textures of the fabrics as a way of bringing interest and a tactile quality to the table. The linen cloth, with its integral, woven square pattern, makes a subtle background, and the vintage French cloth around the bread follows the theme.

The Perfect Breakfast

These days it is rare to get time to enjoy a leisurely breakfast with a friend or partner, so when the opportunity does arise we should make the most of it. First of all think of ease and comfort—well-upholstered chairs, plenty of room to spread out the newspapers, good light to read by, and a radio somewhere in the background so that conversation is not essential.

I usually set the breakfast table the night before, so that it is ready and requires no effort in the morning. I also squeeze some plump grapefruits and oranges and place the juice in attractive vessels in my refrigerator to chill overnight. The setting is supremely simple but the few pieces I use are of good quality, such as crisp linen napkins and hand-decorated studio stoneware plates. I use dinner plates because each is big enough to serve as a tray, a plate, and a saucer, so you aren't left with dreary piles of dishes to wash—which is never a good way to start the day.

It is amusing to think "outside the box" and to use wonderful old linen tea towels or large polka-dot handkerchiefs in place of regular napkins. There are many classic ways of folding napkins, too: The water lily, the slipper, and the fan are just a few of the styles that would have appeared on well-dressed Victorian tables. But I like a napkin to look as though it is ready for use, so I generally choose simple rolls or folds. A napkin can be an ideal place to make a personal welcome to a guest, by writing their name on a luggage tag and tying it on, or even by embroidering it with their name.

Simple touches, such as wrapping the warm bread in a nineteenth-century French napkin before laying it in a shallow basket, and decanting local honey, homemade jam, and butter into glass or ceramic pots, make all the difference. Don't forget to provide a butter knife and a spoon for each jam or honey.

As well as a small potted plant in a decorative container, I have added a bowl of delicious ripe fruit as an edible table decoration. Fruit and flowers can be used to bring a seasonal touch to the table. A winter breakfast, for

above: Each napkin has been rolled up and inserted into two horn rings, one at either end. The top ring is also used to hold the knife in place, creating a compact arrangement. The whole setting has a rustic simplicity but it is clean and crisp, adding a touch of class.

opposite: A large wide-bowl cup allows you to breathe in the delicious aroma of good coffee, stimulating the senses of both smell and taste. Traditionally, the French drink their breakfast coffee or hot chocolate from a bowl, wrapping their hands around its warm exterior.

example, might feature a pot of Christmas roses and a bowl of tangerines;

in autumn, a basket of crisp red apples and blackberries with a vase of

late-flowering roses; and for summer, a dish of freshly picked raspberries

and strawberries with a few sweet peas in a tall glass.

The thing I love most about a breakfast like this is that the smell of warming

bread and good coffee drifts through the house and under bedroom doors,

so even the late risers will find it difficult to linger under the sheets for long.

CHAPTER THREE

About Color

Color is a powerful and versatile decorative
tool that can be used in many ways—both
tonally and in combinations—to create
different moods, themes, and effects.

left: The decoration of this room is plain and understated, in muted neutral tones, providing a simple backdrop for a table ablaze with vivid color.

right: Because the palette of colors is limited, I have incorporated pieces with as much texture as possible.

Mediterranean Blues

Blue is a color I associate most strongly with the south of France—it reminds me of the vivid turquoise sea and the cloudless azure sky. Blue is also a hue that features in all styles and periods of tableware, from eighteenth-century Chinese ceramics to the Bristol blue glass of the early nineteenth century and, as seen here, in a crisp and contemporary placement.

Although my palette of colors for this table is limited to predominantly blue with splashes of white and lemon, I have introduced different tones and plenty of texture in banded and patterned crystal glasses, dimpled-glass candle lanterns, and a vase with a drizzled finish. The cut and dipped surface of the glass reacts beautifully in the flickering golden candlelight, transforming a tumbler into a jeweled vessel and a vase into a glittering orb.

87

top left: The navy blue napkins were decorated with textured leather key fobs in the shape of the initials of the guests, to whom they were given as a parting gift.

top right: This table is set for supper on a hot summer's evening. As the light fades and the candles flicker in the breeze, the intense azure of the textured glass and tableware really comes to life.

bottom right: A large cream napkin with a navy border is folded into a simple square and the furled blue napkin and flatware with

glamorous rock-crystal handles are placed on top at a jaunty angle, giving an unexpected dimension to the arrangement.

bottom left: When color is the unifying element of a scheme, everything does not need to match. Combining glassware in different tones, patterns, and finishes can be very effective.

opposite: The dark wooden table has been waxed and polished, so the surface reflects the candlelight, adding to the play of light in the room and enhancing the colors of the china and glass.

left: Although the setting is predominantly many different shades of blue, I have added brilliant white plates, a large white dish of lemons, and vases of white lilac to enhance the feeling of freshness and vitality.

opposite: The colors and embellishments of the table setting are carried through to the mantelpiece. This trick of echoing the table design elsewhere makes the mantelpiece an integral and valuable component of the overall appearance of the room.

STICKY FINGERS

For a meal of seafood, artichokes, or anything that involves using the hands to shell, peel, or dissect food, I lay two table napkins at each setting. The first napkin is to tuck in at the neck to protect a shirt or blouse, while the other is for the lap and hands. A crystal finger bowl of tepid water decorated with a flower petal or a strip of citrus zest is also a useful aid.

Bitter Orange

Color, scale, and texture are fundamental to the arrangement of this sparkling array of crystal, silver, and china. The centerpiece is a large crystal vase of long-stemmed anemones raised to a height that makes it easy for guests to converse "under" the table arrangement. The vibrant colors of the flowers are followed through at different levels—from the rose petals and capsicums in the base of the glass hurricane candle shades to the individual flower heads in the bud vases at each place setting, to the charger plates and napkins.

A recessed ceiling spot shines soft light directly onto the table and through the cut crystal, casting delicate and ornate patterns across the surface. The crystal also twinkles in the flickering light from the candles around the base of the vase.

Color is a key to this setting and because the room is dark it can cope with an intense splash of strong tones. As the dining chairs are burnt orange, this was an obvious color with which to begin.

The design of the hurricane shades on the table was inspired by a crystal stand used for carving ham.
I loved the shape and thought it would translate well into a crystal base for a generous-size shade.

HURRICANE SHADES

A hurricane shade can be filled with many things, plus a little fine sand in the base to stabilize the candle. I mixed capsicum peppers with rose petals, but you could use pebbles and shells, nuts or crystal chandelier drops, or you could coil handfuls of green rushes or other long pliable stems around the base.

opposite: The flowers and chargers both follow the orange theme but the napkins are a different shade at each place setting—from deep burnt orange to pale primrose yellow. The tones work together harmoniously because they come from the same "family" of color, each with some yellow in its composition.

right: At a large table it can be practical as well as hospitable to place decanters of wine and water at intervals, to be shared by a group of three or four guests. This way, guests can look after themselves when glasses run low and it saves the host having to get up and go around the table refilling glasses.

below: A cut-crystal plate looks like a sunburst when set against the backdrop of a bright orange charger.

Jewel Shades

A ny room lit entirely by candlelight has a magical theatrical feel. But to dine in this room—in which every plane is lavishly decorated and adorned, every inch of the deep crown molding is distressed and gilded, and every surface glows in the flickering candlelight—is to experience a feeling of total opulence.

The colors of topaz, amethyst, tourmaline, and gold are used to full and gracious advantage in this palace of flickering light. My friend and owner of this dining room is a master of decorating. I selected plain white linen mats, which allow the wonderful figuring and grain of the wooden table to be seen. This rich surface frames and highlights the polished crystal and shining silver, which can sometimes become secondary in an elaborate array of cloth, napkins, and embellishment.

left: Never worry about using too many flowers. Here, roses, irises, and sweet peas, in wonderful shades of purples and pinks, are displayed on glittering crystal stands and in fluted vases.

opposite: Order and proportion are provided by crisp white linen place mats that form the structure of this table setting.

SPACING AND PLACING

When arranging a table, make sure there is adequate room around it for people to come easily to their seats and to leave them. If you'll have staff serving, you need to allow space for them to pass behind each occupied chair. Traditionally, the host and hostess take the seats at the head and foot of the table, with guests along the sides, but I like to sit in the middle of my guests, so that I can help conversation along and keep an eye on the removal and filling of plates and glasses. It's fun to place people beside someone they like or know, although they should be courteous enough to invite others to join in their conversation rather than just gossiping among themselves. Adventurous hosts often place people who don't know each other, but who have common interests or have traveled to similar areas, side by side.

top left: A jewel-colored flute of deep amethyst crystal will enhance the pleasure of drinking champagne with a hot fruit soufflé served for dessert.

center left: Rosemary, a herb with healing properties and a delicate refreshing scent, is mixed with deep purple irises to enhance the ambience of the room.

left: Fine honeycomb porcelain candle shades diffuse the candlelight to magical effect.

above: Dark pink lilies decadently strewn on crystal dishes with a few sprigs of rosemary create a truly opulent vision.

opposite: The pineapple is a symbol of welcome and hospitality. Here, crystal pineapples with gilded leaves form part of a splendid display that greets guests as they enter the room.

previous page: The orderly setting of this generous table brings an intimate structure to the bejeweled dining room.

About Gold, White, and Cranberry

Decorating a table for friends can be a great chance to make the most of the innate drama of a well-designed table. This glorious mix of gold, white, and cranberry is opulent but fresh. I love the idea of a great eighteenth-century French table, loaded with monogrammed linens, beautiful hand-painted porcelains, and shiny family silver, looking rich but delicate. The setting works here, too; my friend's dining room is covered with lovely stone and boasts a splendid gilt chandelier.

102

Icreated this French-style table for friends of mine who live nearby. They were having eight to dinner and wanted a glamorous, sophisticated look. The key starting points were already in place: the huge wooden table, the dusky pink upholstered chairs, the gold chandelier, and the gilt mirror. Gold screams glamour while the wooden table is roughly rustic—a wonderful combination in this setting, but one that presented a possible clash of styles for the look I wanted. I solved the problem by covering the table with a crisp white linen cloth—a linen sheet would do just as well. I then kept it simple, with classic silverware, eighteenth-century inspired hand-painted gilded plates, white linen napkins, and cranberry and amethyst glass. The flowers were cut hydrangeas, with pretty detail on each napkin provided by a rose petal.

below left to right and opposite: Once I decide on the palette, I take the colors "through" the table in the glass, china, table linen, or flowers. This look is opulent, but I maintained a modern and informal feel by using a mixture of vintage glass and silver, including cranberry and amethyst water goblets. Scattered flowers, particularly orchids, shriek luxury, while a single petal at each place is a sign that care has been taken.

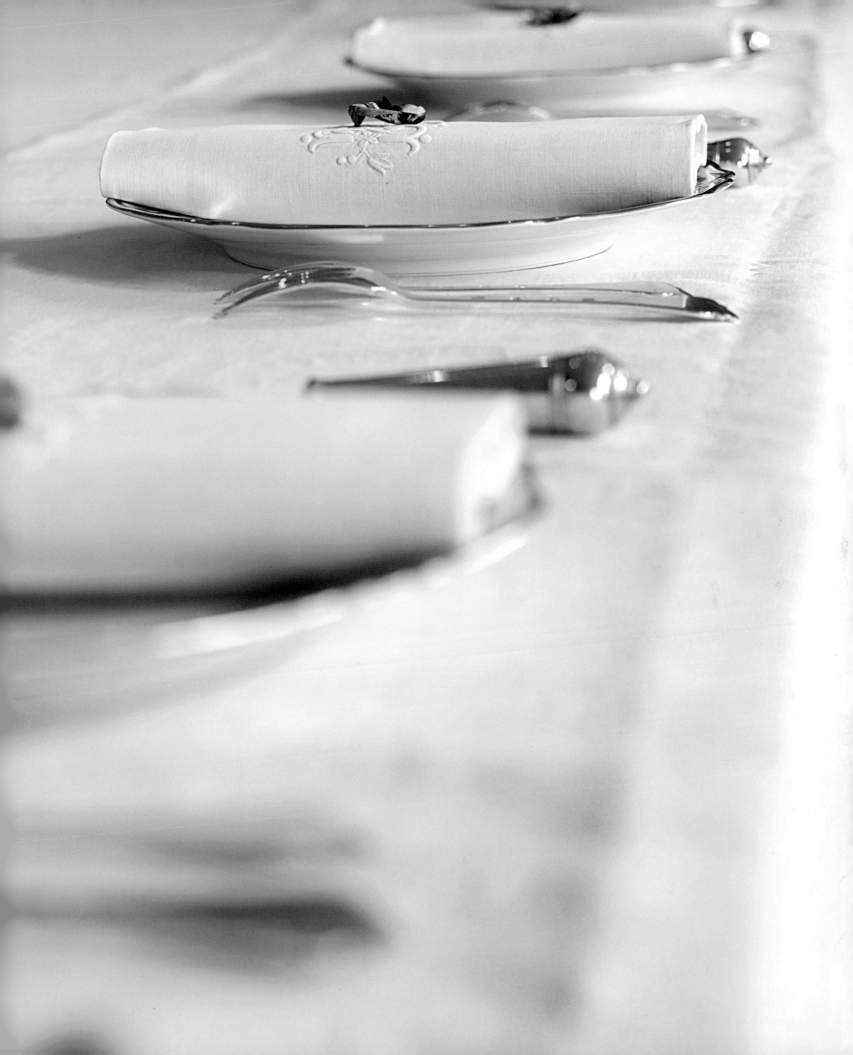

left: A tazza is a heavenly device for making even everyday items look special. Adding bright daisies to a bunch of grapes on the sideboard has helped to bring out the colors of the table.

opposite: To change the look, you can arrange flatware in the French manner with the tips of the fork tines facing down. Gilt makes a reliably glossy statement.

previous page: When creating any table setting, it's important to make sure that guests can easily reach everything they are likely to need, but without making the table feel overly cluttered.

left: An antique Indian organdie sari shawl beaded and embroidered with heavenly hues of amethyst and rose is added as a delicate overcloth to one of plain white linen.

right: Scented roses, peonies, and night-scented stocks subtly fill the air with the sweetest of summer fragrances.

Mother's Lunch

Without question, the most important people in anyone's life are one's parents, and to pay special tribute to an adored mother is particularly satisfying. Whether it be on a birthday, on Mother's Day, or just to say thank you, it is worth taking a little extra time to make it a memorable event and in some small way to show appreciation for the years of comfort, advice, and love that she has shared with you.

A friend asked me to dream up a gorgeous table for a special lunch she was having with her sisters in honor of their adored mother, a lady with whom she has a deeply pleasing and warm relationship. To oblige, I brought together a feminine festival of rose pink, gossamer-light beaded and embroidered organdie, and sparkling crystal to give the occasion a magical touch. A generous scattering of pink rose petals completed the look. The place settings were close together on this compact round table to bring intimacy to this wonderfully private event.

below left: A furl of gauzy pink ribbon and a scattering of rose petals augment the beauty of a tazza of freshly baked macaroons. Lifting food off the table with a tazza or a piece of stemmed glassware creates a glamorous effect.

below: The heads of large peonies nestle against the rim of their cut-crystal vases.

opposite: A girl's beaded bracelet makes an enchanting napkin ring and brings color to the table and plate.

NAPKIN RINGS

I like to think laterally when it comes to wrapping or tying napkins. Ideas vary from simple garden twine with luggage labels or white flower buds to sophisticated silver rings, beaded bracelets, or hair-tie pom-poms. I find that napkin rings provide a great opportunity to introduce a little humor to the table.

CHAPTER FOUR

Natural Hues

Take inspiration from the natural world around you—from warm earthy tones to cool whites, blues, and greens—and use these colors to create unique and stylish table settings.

Tête à Tête

This table is about conversation and creating time and space to catch up with a friend. To achieve this goal I placed the table in an area of peace and tranquility away from the hustle, bustle, and distractions of the household. The small table is positioned by a window overlooking the garden, which gives a feeling of being somewhere secluded and out of the way.

An elegant pitcher of water with two glasses, some decorative condiment holders, a simple butter dish, and a pair of attractive

above: This napkin is folded in an elegant step design, and the bone-handled fruit knife and fork are laid separately on the individual folds of the cloth. Fruit knives and forks like these work equally well for a crisp salad.

below: Placing the chairs with their backs to the room and putting them side by side helps increase the feeling of intimacy. The focus of attention is outward, to the walled garden, rather than inward to the room.

below left and top right: Decorative condiment holders and small ancillary dishes contribute to the overall appearance of the table—they are useful objects but have an intrinsic beauty, too.

below right: A fine glass can make the most mundane drink seem exciting. Even if you are only serving water with lunch, it is still worthwhile serving it in an elegant glass.

center right: I enjoy fine craftsmanship even in its simplest form, such as a couple of decorative rows of embroidery or a band of pattern woven into the edge of cloth: it makes something ordinary become special.

dinner plates are all that are required. Because the focus of the lunch is closeness and conversation, I have kept the table decorations low and minimal: just a small posy of anemones to complement the double row of embroidery along the border of the vintage linen cloth. As this is a casual, informal lunch for close friends, the bread can be broken and left on the side of the plate or on the table—it helps to encourage a feeling of intimacy.

opposite: A foldaway card table is ideal for serving tea—the dishes are not very heavy, so the table doesn't need to be as robust as one used for formal dining.

right: In spring, when flowers are still scarce, I like to augment cut flowers with those grown in pots in my greenhouse.

Fireside Tea

To me, this is a perfect culmination to a Saturday afternoon in the country. After some energetic gardening or a brisk walk with the dog, you come indoors to a delicious fireside tea. The institution of having tea hasn't changed much since my childhood and I like to capture that feeling of nostalgia and times gone by with traditional blue and white Spode china and plenty of homemade jams, cakes, and cookies.

The skill is to keep a relaxed feeling, to make it appear as though tea has arrived effortlessly. The setting is therefore undemanding and based on a layering of pattern on pattern. I started with the vintage blue and white checked cotton cloth, laid with the patterned china, a Georgian silver teapot and milk jug, and a little pot of spring flowers. To finish, I added embroidered napkins pulled through a child's elasticized bracelet, which makes a perfect, jolly napkin ring.

opposite: Blue and white china and table linen have a crisp, clean, fresh look, which enhances the appearance of food that is placed upon it. There are many china patterns found in this blue and white coloring, the most popular being the Willow pattern and Spode Italian, as seen here. The term "Willow" was applied to many types of blue and white porcelain imported from China during the late eighteenth century. For more than 150 years the Willow pattern has been made by a wide range of British pottery manufacturers, such as Minton, Spode, and Royal Worcester.

below left: The vintage embroidered design on the napkin, of a merry farmer and his woolly sheep, is a humorous reference to the countryside walk from which we have just returned. I often buy odd pairs or numbers of napkins, if that is all that I can find, because they can be used for small gatherings, such as this, or individually as tray cloths.

below center: Glass or crystal "confiture" pots allow their contents to tantalize the taste buds. The golden glint of honey or burgundy richness of strawberry jam will tempt all who see them.

below right: Drawn-thread work, where single or pairs of threads are removed from the fabric to reveal a small decorative opening, and overstitching, such as chainstitch or herringbone stitch, were popular needlework embellishments for tea cloths and napkins in Victorian times.

SERVING WITH STYLE

I believe that it is worth taking that little extra time to decant honey and jam into attractive pots or dishes.

This makes them look so much more appealing and appetizing than serving them in screw-top jars with a commercial label across the front. Even if you haven't made your own jam, manufactured conserves look more wholesome if well displayed. Providing individual spoons for each pot avoids an unappetizing mix of confections, while a traditional wooden or ceramic dipper, with its rounded and ribbed surface, is perfect for serving "runny" honey.

Perfect White

This simple but charming table setting is ideal for lunch or for a casual supper with friends or close family. It is pretty, stylish, and perfect for entertaining any age group. The table is very easy to arrange, making this straightforward setting ideal for a young couple or newlyweds to undertake when hosting their first meal together. All that's needed are a few basic but carefully chosen elements to put the look together.

White china, elegant crystal, and vintage linen napkins are placed around antique pewter chargers, whose worn surfaces complement the well-used tabletop with its rich patina and act as a foil to the pristine white linen and china. The folded napkins form a background for the silverware, and delicate flower buds could be used to highlight the fine embroidery on the fabric surface.

In keeping with the country location and informal style of this room, I created a simple table setting based on white and clear glassware, with the wonderful worn surface of the old wooden table as a backdrop.

By keeping the setting uncomplicated and monotone, the food that is brought to the table becomes the focus of attention—its color, texture, and aroma will be the key features. For this reason, on occasions such as this I am especially careful when selecting my ingredients at the market. I search out the most handsome pears, the crispest lettuce, the most mouthwatering ripe strawberries.

This simple white table setting also makes a good base or starting point for creating a scheme with touches of color. You can follow this basic style but then add a signature or feature color, such as pink napkins and rosebuds, or green chargers and napkins tied with fronds of lemongrass, giving just a subtle hint of color.

below left: A crisp green salad with a variety of colors and types of leaves looks good in a simple glass bowl.

below center: I introduced tiny vases of buds to the side of each plate to make the first course of chilled soup appear more exciting (see page 126); when the first course was cleared away, the vases of flowers were arranged in a group on the mantelshelf.

below right: The aesthetic impact of a well-arranged table napkin is undeniable. Whether plain or beautifully embroidered, a well-laundered linen or cotton square can be a backdrop to flatware or further enhanced by a ring, ribbon, or single flower.

opposite: If you have a long table but are inviting only a few people to dinner, use large vases of flowers to screen off the end of the table and make it feel more intimate. Here, I grouped together three hurricane shades, usually used to hold candles but equally attractive with large bunches of long-stemmed flowers.

opposite: I like to leave simple fare and fine ingredients to bask in their own glory—just a plain glass bowl or dish, or a neutral-colored plate is all that is required. Here, an antique pewter charger complements the aged surface of the table and an unadorned white plate highlights the color of the chilled soup set upon it.

below: When a fruit is in season, there is nothing more delicious than enjoying it at its peak of perfection. There is a trick that designers and stylists often use of arranging things in odd numbers—for example, a group of three is often more visually pleasing than four. Here, a group of seven pears fits perfectly inside the rim of the plate; the pear grouping, salad, and plate of strawberries add up to a total of three.

THE DINING TABLE

A dining table must be adequate in size for the number of guests you are inviting and for the number of dishes and courses that you intend to serve. Ideally, you should try to place everything that you and your guests will need on the table, so there must be sufficient room to accommodate these items without the overall effect looking cluttered. If necessary, take a course-by-course approach and only bring to the table what you need for each course and clear it away before the next.

In terms of shape, round tables are useful because they can accommodate an odd number of people more easily and less noticeably. A round table also encourages conversation to flow around it, rather than across it or at an angle, as is often the way at a rectangular table. On the other hand, rectangular tables are more readily extended and reduced to cope with varying numbers of guests.

Apartment Dining

The challenge of apartment living is, invariably, to make the most of the space you have. Here, the evening starts with drinks and canapés served on the terrace, with the wine transported in an elegant leather carrier. The table inside is set with crisp black leather mats, which give a chic metropolitan air to the plain wood table. To add interest, I laid two mats at each place—a large one for the plate and a smaller one, at the left-hand side, for the flatware.

The palette of colors is limited to the brown and blue tones of the contemporary studio-pottery plates. The glassware is also understated and without surface decoration. To add dignity and a little grandeur, I placed an unusual nineteenth-century bronze candelabra in the center of the table and had the guests' names embroidered on their napkins.

Crisp black leather place mats complement the stylish dining chairs and bring a sleek metropolitan appearance to the plain wooden table.

opposite: Studio-made glazed terra-cotta tableware is informal but can be made to appear more sophisticated when arranged on stitched leather mats. Leather is a good heat-resistant material for place mats, but it should be wiped clean after each use and, every couple of months, treated with a leather food and polished to maintain its handsome appearance.

below: It is easier to carry a number of bottles separately than on a tray, as they can be heavy and make the tray unbalanced. Here, a leather bottle "bucket" holds bottles of white and red wine, cassis, and water, so they can be effortlessly transported to the terrace.

FEAST FACTS

Dinner has been part of sociable life since the time of the Ancient Greeks and Romans, a chance to be merry and to enjoy good food and drink. In early times a dinner was held to celebrate a god's feast day or a birthday, or on occasions of public rejoicing. In England, the art of cooking was not noted much before the reign of Elizabeth I, and it was in the reign of Charles II that the fare became more refined and delicate, with recipes for pigeon pie and strawberry cake dating from that time. Now, in the twenty-first century, food has become global, with a worldwide repertoire focusing on fewer courses and good-quality ingredients.

Provençal Lunch

To me, this is an honest table with earthiness and purity, yet it encompasses a spectrum of natural shades—the deep glaze of the candlesticks and plant pots, the honey wood, the biscuit place mats, the creamy pottery and napkins. Each and every detail of the setting is beautiful, like a still-life painting. The textures are a balance of coarse and smooth—the polished wooden table and smooth glazed pottery juxtaposed with the rough linen mats. Wine and water are served in a stoneware pitcher and bottle; the candlesticks complement the hand-thrown earthenware plates.

opposite: It would be inappropriate to have ornate cut-crystal glasses on this table, as they would look thoroughly out of place. Instead, I have used rustic hand-blown glasses, each a little different from the next but in keeping with the handmade pottery and the antique linen cloths in which the wholesome bread is wrapped.

below: The individual cheese plates are part of a set especially made by a prestigious local potter. The traditional French *planche,* or platter, can also be made of wood and is often used when eating simple fare such as bread and cheese or a croissant. For storage it can be hung on a wooden peg on the wall.

Instead of using cut flowers I selected potted bulbs. I think this is especially appropriate for spring flowers, because once you have enjoyed this year's blooms you can plant the bulbs in the garden or in tubs on the balcony and enjoy them when they bloom again the following year.

This style of simple rustic setting reminds me of being on vacation among the lavender fields of Provence, eating fine French cheeses and freshly baked baguettes, washed down with a glass of good locally produced wine. Even when I come home, I find it therapeutic and relaxing to re-create a meal that captures that feeling of carefree enjoyment.

above: Although the glassware on the table is simple, more stylish champagne bowls can be used to serve champagne as an aperitif.

opposite: The earthenware bottle and pitcher are visually pleasing and can easily be filled with wine, water, or cordial and chilled in the fridge, as necessary.

previous page: Although this rustic setting is in rural England it has a very French feel—the natural colors and the simplicity and quality of the materials and tableware help to impart that continental ambience.

below left: A small paper luggage label tied around the monogrammed napkin with string makes a perfect place card. The rough string complements the place mat, and both are set against the smooth napkin and glazed plate.

below: If liquid is decanted into the pottery bottles in advance, so that the containers are chilled with the contents, they will keep it cooler for longer when placed on the table.

Breakfast Tray

Sometimes a friend will arrive unexpectedly or at short notice and stay for a night; thankfully the guest room is always prepared. The following morning, to make them feel especially welcome and to start their day on a good note, I like to present my guests with an uncomplicated wake-up tray.

The modern zinc tray that I usually use is large enough to rest safely on your lap in bed. I cover the surface with a crisp square of linen; the cloth doesn't have to be the same size and shape as the tray because it is more to do with the quality and appearance than the fit. As I have drawers full of "favorite" small linen cloths and single napkins, I love the opportunity to select a couple of special pieces and put them on show.

SAFETY FIRST

If serving a hot drink such as tea on a breakfast tray, insure that a heat-absorbent mat is placed beneath the pot, otherwise the heat will seep through the tray and could give an unpleasant shock to someone resting it on their lap or placing their arm underneath it. Another tip is to use a slightly larger pot than necessary and to underfill it, so that the hot liquid will not splash out while being carried.

opposite: An unpretentious little glass filled with fresh flowers and a pretty plate with a gilded edge are all that are needed to turn a tray into a hospitable and gracious greeting.

right: I find a small, unstable tray and crumbly food a nuisance in bed, but a good-size tray or one with legs that fit comfortably over your legs makes the whole experience even more enjoyable.

Drawn-thread work and crocheted borders give well-laundered antique linens the extra delicacy and charm that make them so appealing.

Tea at Four

I have drawers full of pieces of vintage linen such as small cloths, mats, and unmatched napkins, and they come into their own when a friend comes to visit for tea and cake. Tea is a pleasant, calming institution that helps to revive body and soul in mid-afternoon.

One good teaspoon of leaves is sufficient to make two cups of tea. The pot should first be prewarmed with a little hot water, which is then thrown away. The tea leaves are placed in the pot, and the hot water poured over them and left to brew for three to four minutes before pouring. Always make sure that you have a tea-leaf strainer and small bowl handy.

TEATIME TREATS

I often buy lemon or chocolate cakes from local produce fairs or garden fêtes and put them in the freezer, so that they can be used for an unexpected tea or for a treat. Fruitcake is another useful thing to keep in the pantry; it can last for weeks in an airtight container. Even store-bought cakes can be given a "homemade" appearance by dusting them with confectioner's sugar or cocoa powder.

I covered this wooden tray with a plain white linen cloth with a decorative border and added a stack of white embroidered napkins to catch the crumbs. I chose old white china cups and side plates with an understated red rim, which complements the red of the floral pillow and is highlighted by the roses in the small bud vase. As I have a limited supply of this particular pattern of china, I supplemented the side plates with delicate glass dishes that tie in with the glass cake stand. I find that antique fruit knives are ideal for serving a dainty slice of cake dusted with confectioner's sugar.

opposite: A glass cake stand helps to raise even a small cake to grander heights and a plain stand can be dressed with a cloth to give it extra presence. Use a stand with a flat surface for presenting food that needs to be sliced, such as cake, and save stands with a dish or bowl for serving fruit.

right: Teas of the finest flavor are made from the younger leaves of the tea plant, and as a drink for the afternoon I prefer a good Indian or Ceylon variety. The scented teas, such as Earl Grey and the more mellow Lady Grey, which both contain bergamot, are also delicious and refreshing.

opposite: A basket-weave crystal wine cooler makes a fine container for a generous bouquet of white and cream flowers.
right: A crystal decanter of malt whiskey, cognac, or a fortified wine such as port or sherry is an inviting sight on a well-arranged tray.

Cocktails at Home

B efore going to the theater or even after a concert or dinner at a restaurant it is enjoyable to invite friends home for cocktails. Make the occasion special by having a tray prepared with a starched white linen cloth, a generous vase of flowers, and an array of beautifully polished glasses. A few hors d'oeuvres are always a welcome accompaniment, but keep them simple and light so that they don't dull your appetite or make your guests feel overly full.

WASHING GLASS AND CRYSTAL

When it comes to washing glass and crystal, I don't think any of the modern washing and rinsing products can beat a bowl of warm soapy water. Wash crystal glasses one at a time and rinse them in clean tepid water. Be careful when taking glasses out of a sink not to knock them against a faucet. Leave the glasses to drain but not dry, then polish them with a lintfree cloth or linen glass towel. If you leave glasses to dry on a draining board they often become marked by water drips or dribbles.

The Essentials

FORWARD PLANNING

I am a great believer in organizing and doing as much as possible in advance because I like to have time to relax before my guests arrive. I also set aside time for the things that can only be done moments before the doorbell rings. But it's important to relax and be flexible, and to allow for changes, interruptions, and even the odd mishap or oversight on the shopping list.

A table setting should enhance but not dominate a course or dish. Choose colors, flowers, fruit, flatware, china, crystal, and glass that will frame and augment the food and drink that you serve, rather than overpower and diminish it. And don't feel you have to use all your china and glassware at once; you can set a very crisp and elegant table with a few well-chosen pieces. Equally, only set out the utensils that are needed; if your table is small, you might consider clearing them away with each course and bringing fresh utensils with the following dish.

The table dressing should always be appropriate to the occasion. I often suggest to friends who are anxious about planning a setting that they think of dressing a table in the same way as they think about dressing themselves; you wouldn't wear the same clothes to the grocery store as you would to a nightclub, for example. So, think about who is coming, what the event is for, and the type of food you are serving, and take your lead from there.

In certain circumstances the event itself may suggest a color or theme. For instance, a christening lunch party, which celebrates the beginning of a new life, should be fresh and light and may include pink or blue as appropriate to the gender of the child. Birthdays can be influenced by the season in which they occur: Summer parties benefit from loose arrangements of freshly picked flowers, and autumnal events from decorations featuring amber, nut brown, and gold; winter celebrations can focus on the crisp greenness of pine and the frosty whiteness of snow, but with red, silver, or gold for a festive twist. Wedding anniversaries are often celebrated with gifts of a specific material, such as crystal, silver, ruby, gold, or diamond, and these can be used as a theme. Ruby, emerald, and sapphire may be precious stones but they are also wonderful colors that can be picked out in flowers and napkins, or in the crystal or glassware.

Aim to distribute color from top to bottom on the table, from tall candles or flowers down to the china and the trim of the napkin or cloth. Balance color, too, leaving a breathing space of a white or glass plate or bowl, so that the mix of tones and hues is not overpowering.

TIP

I am often asked how I know when to stop adding things to a table, and my answer is, "stop when there's one more thing you want to do." Avoid fussy trimmings and clutter—people need room around their plate, whether to raise a glass and put it down again, to unfurl a napkin, or to lift and use flatware.

WHERE TO BEGIN

THE SETTING ORDER

● Choose your table and location. You don't always have to dine in the dining room or kitchen—it can be interesting to have a cozy dinner *à deux* by the fireside or a lunch with a friend in a sitting room or in the bay of a window. The table should be an appropriate size for the number of people being entertained, but if you only have a large table and there are just two of you, then set one end or side of the table with a small cloth and sit beside each other, so that it doesn't feel as though you were expecting more guests to arrive.

● Remove the chairs from around the table, or don't bring them to the table until you have finished arranging the places. Chairs hinder your access and make it more difficult and time-consuming to set the table, especially if the chairs have high backs.

● Make sure the table surface is clean and, if it's wooden and no cloth is being used, polish it. For a lunch party, polish the table the night before and for a dinner party, during the morning. By doing this you will leave time for the wax to soak in and be rubbed off, although it is worth giving a final buff just before you set the table because any residue on the surface can become marked. Preparing the table early also allows time for the smell of the polish or wax to disperse.

● Set out the base, whether it is a cloth, runner, mats, or charger plates. Place chargers or individual mats in front of where the chairs will go to denote the position of each guest.

● Always work in strict rotation to avoid missing a piece of the table setting.

● Add the glassware, starting with a stemmed wine glass, if appropriate, and placing a water glass beside it. Polish each with a lintfree cloth.

● Polish and arrange the flatware.

● Roll or fold the napkins, whatever best suits your setting.

● Stand back from the table and take an overview. When working on individual place settings, it is difficult to get a balanced vision of the whole arrangement.

● Add candles, making sure they will be easy to light and not too close to the diners.

● Add place cards and final napkin embellishments such as labels, rings, or cord ties.

● Leave the room, have coffee, or do something else for a few moments, then return to the table afresh and you will be able to see where things are out of line or if something is missing.

● I put flowers on the table at the last moment, partly because the room will be warm and could cause the flowers to open or droop and partly to keep the cloth or table surface as pristine as possible. Individual buds on napkins need to be positioned just before the guests come to the table because the buds have to survive without water. Then take a final overview from a distance.

● A few moments before the guests come to the table, light the candles.

TIP

Once your guests have all arrived, turn off your cell phone and put the answering machine on for the house phone, so that you won't be distracted from your role of host or hostess. Your sole focus should be those in your company, not others elsewhere. And, as a guest, turn your phone off on arrival; if you are expecting an urgent call, turn the phone to vibrate mode rather than ring.

CHINA AND TABLEWARE

I have enough plates to serve dinner to 100 without borrowing anything, but then I have to confess to being something of a collector—or a hoarder. I have eight main services of china that I use regularly, with other, smaller sets that I use from time to time. Don't forget that, above all, entertaining is about the people you have invited and they matter most—if we had people and no plates, we'd manage, but if we had plates and no people, it would be no fun at all!

THE BASIC RANGE

I would advise any host or hostess to have a good basic *mise en place*—a set of plates and bowls in a single color that you can use time and again and that allows you to create different looks with the addition of flowers, napkins, and trimmings. This style of plate may be unadorned white or cream, but it doesn't have to be dull—it could have a rim of raised rings or a subtly scalloped edge, or some other detail that reflects your personality and suits you.

Versatility is the key to a basic range. Find the shape and depth of bowl that you can use to serve soup, salad, pasta, and dessert, as well as breakfast cereal. A standard dinner plate is 10in (25cm), a dessert plate is 8in (20cm), and a side plate is 6in (15cm); you can serve just about any combination of courses on these. A 13in (33cm) charger makes a great alternative to a place mat and, if in a contrasting color to the main plate, adds a decorative element. Chargers and larger plates, however, may not fit into the dishwasher and will have to be washed by hand.

To dress up the basic range I would have several smaller sets of decorative dishes and plates, just enough to serve all your guests on the same patterned or colored plate for one course.

TYPES OF TABLEWARE

The most chic tableware is usually fine English bone china or French porcelain, and these materials are most often used in formal dinner services, either bought as a wedding present or handed down through a family. In addition, most homes will have an everyday range of basic household pottery that can be put in a microwave or dishwasher without being harmed.

I also have handmade studio plates, which I love to place on an antique linen cloth for a lunch or supper of homemade bread, delicious cheeses, and a good wholesome soup—stoneware and earthenware are appropriately rustic for this type of occasion. Other staples in my china closet are glass and crystal plates, which can be used beside or on top of any type of china. Because they are light and transparent, they help give an appearance of space and light on the table.

Where appropriate I will use dishes or plates associated with the country or culture that has inspired the menu—for example, small porcelain bowls, chopsticks, and ceramic spoons for an Oriental dinner or hand-thrown terra-cotta plates for an Italian feast.

I am wholeheartedly behind the idea of mixing different wares, as long as everyone is served the course on the same plate. You could, for example, bring soup to the table in a colored bowl, and follow by serving the main course on a white plate, with salad on a crystal or glass side plate; dessert could be on a decorated fruit plate or in a stemmed glass. I also find it perfectly acceptable to mix gold- and silver-rimmed tableware but would avoid using platinum. (Unless specifically designed to withstand the temperature and chemicals of a dishwasher, gilded dishes should be washed by hand.) Above all, don't be governed by what it says on the box—a vessel is a container and can be used for containing or transporting many different things.

FLATWARE

The basic canteen of domestic flatware will have six to twelve table knives, table forks, dessert/cheese knives, dessert forks, dessert spoons, soup spoons, and teaspoons, with a pair of serving spoons. Traditional canteens also used to have fish knives and forks as well as fruit knives and forks, but these are not often used in modern households. More recent additions to the canteen are steak knives and forks, the knife having a serrated edge that makes it more suitable for cutting thick meat. Where a soup spoon is not available, a serving spoon can be substituted.

Decorative spoons, such as those with colorful enamel insets or handles embedded with semiprecious stones, are often set aside for coffee but I use them for sorbet or small, delicate desserts. I also like to have a set of knives and forks that are slightly smaller than those for the main course, to use for salads and hors d'oeuvres. I often use antique fruit knives and forks for a cheese course and have a selection of unusual pieces such as spoons and utensils made from polished coconut shell, lacquer, and ceramic that bring a change of pace and texture to the table.

Knife handles come in various finishes, too; as well as traditional silver, electro-plated nickel silver (EPNS), and stainless steel, there is bone, horn, agate, rock crystal, and ebony. Modern composite and resin handles can emulate precious and endangered substances such as ivory and tortoiseshell, as well as coming in strong colors or vivid swirls of myriad shades. Several classic handle designs dating from the eighteenth century are still popular today, including the raised "Rattail," rounded "Bead," plain "Fiddle," and ornate and embossed "Kings." Contemporary streamlined designs are also widely available, many of which are ergonomically designed and have handles with a matte finish rather than a highly polished one.

I strongly recommend that when you are buying flatware, you test it before purchasing. The handles should sit comfortably in your hand, the proportions must be aesthetically pleasing, and the balance should be good, so that the handle isn't overly heavy or the blade too light.

TIP

Classic bone-handle knives should never be put in a dishwasher. They must be washed by hand without allowing the handles to soak too long in the water. This also applies to any knives made in two pieces and "bonded."

ARRANGING FLATWARE

There are a variety of ways to set out flatware. The French favor placing the rounded back of the fork facing the diner, whereas the British place the back on the table. In Edwardian times the dessert spoon and fork, as well as the cheese knife, were set across the top of the placement, but these days there are few formal rules. My feeling is that these pieces are tools for food and that as long as they serve their purpose and are neatly aligned you can choose where you want to put them, provided that they are accessible and obvious.

The classic way to set out and use flatware is from the outside in, so that the implements needed for the first dish are on the outer edges, with the flatware for the remaining courses progressing inward, so that the pieces next to the plate are the last to be used.

CRYSTAL AND GLASSWARE

GLASS USE AND SETTING

Matching glassware can look dull, so I like to mix not just patterns and styles but also colors and finishes. As with mixing china (see page 152), make sure that all guests have the same glass for the same drink, although the decoration may vary.

- Wine glasses should ideally be stemmed; use a large bowl for red wine, a smaller one for white.
- For casual meals I use a tumbler or double old-fashioned glass for water, and for formal occasions a large, colored stemmed glass. In general, I use colored glassware only for water.
- Don't be too worried about "proper" use of glassware. If you have fabulous crystal champagne glasses, use them to serve a crisp chilled white wine; equally, for a casual supper of pasta and salad, a small and simple tumbler can be used for a robust red wine.
- Glassware can multitask. Sherry, liqueur, and brandy glasses and champagne flutes can all double as flower vases—why not float a gardenia head in each?—and stemmed glassware, such as champagne bowls, can be used to serve individual desserts such as fruit compote or mousse.

LINENS

CLOTHS AND MATS

Cotton is widely used for table linens and can be plain or woven with a self-pattern, such as jacquard, where the design appears within the material. Colors can also be woven in or printed onto cotton. As long as the design is colorfast, it can be washed at a high temperature, which is useful for removing stains. Cotton can also be starched for a crisp, immaculate appearance.

Linen is generally heavier than cotton and has a longer life expectancy. Some of my linen tablecloths and napkins date from the 1900s and have a wonderful patina—I never mind if antique linen is monogrammed with others' initials. Linen can be very finely woven, as in fine Irish linen, or more coarsely woven resulting in slub and texture on the surface. Fine linen is ideal for formal entertaining, while the coarser finish is attractive for casual or informal occasions.

Wool is not often used on tables but I love to bring the unexpected to table settings and sometime use a fine wool plaid blanket or a crocheted bed cover (see pages 32, 52, and 62) instead of a cloth. Equally fun can be seersucker fabric or a vintage shawl (see pages 72 and 110).

If the evening is elegant and formal, use a floor-length undercloth that reflects the color of your theme or palette and then add a white cloth over the top. The topper cloth should be a little shorter, so that the undercloth can be seen, like a petticoat under a skirt. As a rule of thumb, make sure the diameter of a circular cloth, or the width and length or a rectangular one, are about 12in (30cm) more than those of the table, so the topper has a drop of about 6in (15cm).

TABLE NAPKINS

For me, napkins are an essential part of table dressing. Not only do they have a practical purpose in protecting your clothes from drips or spills and wiping the mouth and fingers, but they can be used to bring height to a table where the setting is all at the same level, as well as to add color and texture. If you have a simple tablecloth with a few rows of colored stitching around the border, for example, use napkins to highlight that color. Similarly, napkins can be used to echo the color of the flowers or candles. Napkin rings, ties, and decorations also provide endless decorative opportunities (see pages 82 and 112). But please reserve paper napkins for picnics—for all other occasions use only cotton or linen.

FLOWERS

For a special party, I like to put individual flower heads at each place setting. The flowers don't all have to be the same; it can be fun to choose a bloom to suit the character or style of each guest, or to take a head of each of the flowers in the main arrangement. Equally, if you can only find a few jaded blooms, don't despair—put the best heads in small individual bowls or pull off the petals and use them around the base of candles or scattered over the cloth.

TIP

I recommend a basic "wardrobe" of three or four bud vases to hold individual stems, a tall flute vase for a few elegant sprays, and a low vase or deep dish that can be used for a centerpiece. Make sure the container does not clash with your chosen blooms; glass and crystal are safe choices, as they suit every type of flower.

I often use flowers to bring out the color of the tablecloth or napkins—but avoid very strongly scented flowers, as they'll compete with the food and overwhelm your taste buds. I use highly scented flowers only in the entry hall and sitting room—the same applies to scented candles. If I am entertaining in town I sometimes choose a single flower, such as a white rose, and fill a large champagne cooler with dozens of them. In the country I mix the blooms and have a less formal arrangement—it's about encompassing the ambience of the setting and style of entertaining.

Good-looking fruit and vegetables also make a welcoming centerpiece. I like to cut a few pieces of fruit open—but use fruit that won't go brown, such as pomegranates or lemons. Foliage and grasses can also be arranged to make a stunning centerpiece or used to bind a napkin.

CRUETS   Traditionally, cruets were small stoppered bottles that contained condiments, but now the term embraces the containers that hold salt, pepper, mustard, and various accompaniments such as soya and wasabi. Coarse salt is usually presented in a small open dish with a spoon, whereas fine salt can be shaken from a cellar. The same applies to pepper, although for coarse-ground pepper a mill is usually offered. Salt and pepper shakers are often sold in pairs and can be amusingly decorated with characters or figures. These are fun for a casual meal or for a children's setting. For formal occasions, small ceramic or bone dishes, glass bowls, or silver cellars are more appropriate.

INDEX

ACKNOWLEDGMENTS

Without question this, my first book, has been an extremely stimulating and deeply amusing experience. The chance to work with such talent, such humor, and such kindness has been, and will be, my lasting memory.

"Borrow this, take that: look at this, look at that," still rings in my ears.

To those who lent me their wonderful houses there has to be a very special thanks! For the delicious hospitality, beds for the night, and marvellous chatter, I thank you sincerely.

My friends, colleagues, and my wonderful team are the reason that this book has happened at all: "Willie, put it in a book" – so I did just that!

May I thank equally, sincerely, and certainly in no order the following, who are listed here as I so want them all to be thanked by name, some simply for their abstract inspiration!

Joan Golfar

Roger Banks Pye

Min Hogg

Ann Boyd

Tom Blumenthal

Bruce Oldfield

David and Caroline Dickinson

Carol Paul

Roger and Caroline Hall

Joseph and Isabel Ettedgui

Suzanne Rheinstein

Susan Crewe

Simon and Annabel Elliott

Jed Pogran

Melissa Wyndham

Adam Mahr

Alidad Mahloudji

Tim and Dana Jenkins

Miranda Iveagh

Leonie Highton

Nicholas Carter

Gary Cooper

Paul Bramfitt

Nina Campbell

Rupert Thomas

Terence Barry

Angus and Sophie Warre

Margaret Russell

Samantha Kingcome

Vinney Lee

Lisa Gibson-Keynes

Joe Trinanes

Jane Sacchi

Dominique Browning

Tricia Guild

Michael Nicholson

Ali Sharland at Sharland and Lewis

Ant Martens

Aurelie Mathigot

Karen Carroll

Mark Smith

Karen Wilson

Giles Kime

Geoffrey Harley

The Weaver brothers at Guinevere Antiques

Lucy Giles

Christine Wood

Marian McEvoy

Susan de Jesus

Clare Hutchison

Pat Lejuene

Paul Davidson

Adriana Elia

Stephen Woodhams

Thomas Goode and Company

William Yeoward
270 Kings Road
London SW3 5AW
+44 (0)20 7349 7828
www.williamyeoward.com

Thanks to my dear publisher, Cindy Richards, and to my loyal friend and photographer, Ray Main.

And of course lastly, and mostly, Colin.